INVESTIGATING
Conspiracy Theories

Wartime Secrets, Assassination Plots,
AND MORE CONSPIRACY THEORIES ABOUT U.S. HISTORY

by Phillip Simpson

CAPSTONE PRESS
a capstone imprint

Published by Capstone Press, an imprint of Capstone
1710 Roe Crest Drive, North Mankato, Minnesota 56003
capstonepub.com

Copyright © 2025 by Capstone. All rights reserved. No part of this publication may be reproduced in whole or in part, or stored in a retrieval system, or transmitted in any form or by any means, electronic, mechanical, photocopying, recording, or otherwise, without written permission of the publisher.

Library of Congress Cataloging-in-Publication Data is available on the Library of Congress website.
ISBN: 9781669077565 (hardcover)
ISBN: 9781669077510 (paperback)
ISBN: 9781669077527 (ebook PDF)

Summary: Was there a government plot to kill President John F. Kennedy? Did the U.S. government know that the Pearl Harbor attack was going to happen? Conspiracy theories about U.S. history have cropped up since the country formed. Find out why people believe in them and what experts say. Can the conspiracy theories be easily debunked? Or is the truth still waiting to be found?

Editorial Credits
Editor: Carrie Sheely; Designer: Jaime Willems; Media Researcher: Svetlana Zhurkin; Production Specialist: Whitney Schaefer

Image Credits
Capstone: Jaime Willems (doodles), cover, back cover, and throughout; Courtesy of the Federal Bureau of Investigations: 15; Dreamstime: Phillip Kraskoff, 13; Getty Images: Andy_Oxley (airplane), cover, back cover, 1, Central Press, 16, Hulton Archive, 11, 18, Keystone, 21; Library of Congress: cover (bottom left), 10, 14, 26; National Archives and Records Administration: 7; Newscom: Everett Collection, 20, Roll Call/Office of the House Historian, 22, ZUMA Press/The Commercial Appeal/Bob Williams, 19; Shutterstock: AYO Production, 8, BW Folsom, 17, CLS Digital Arts, cover (bottom middle), Everett Collection, 28, Mega Pixel (yellow paper), cover, back cover, and throughout, Nikolay Suchkov (color pins), cover, back cover, and throughout, pics five (string), cover, back cover, and throughout, Skylines (instant photo), cover and throughout; Superstock: Science Photo Library/Victor Habbick Visions, 5; U.S. Naval History and Heritage Command: 27, NARA/U.S. Army Signal Corps, 25

Any additional websites and resources referenced in this book are not maintained, authorized, or sponsored by Capstone. All product and company names are trademarks™ or registered® trademarks of their respective holders.

Printed and bound in China. PO 5827

TABLE OF CONTENTS

Chapter 1
What Are Conspiracy Theories? 4

Chapter 2
The Assassination of John F. Kennedy 10

Chapter 3
The Assassination of Dr. Martin Luther King Jr. 18

Chapter 4
The Pearl Harbor Conspiracy 24

Glossary 30
Read More 31
Internet Sites 31
Index 32
About the Author.. 32

Words in **BOLD** are in the glossary.

Chapter 1

WHAT ARE CONSPIRACY THEORIES?

During World War II (1939–1945), the Allies and the Axis powers fought against each other. Both sides experimented with weapons and technology. Advanced weapons could mean big advantages. Did one experiment make a U.S. Navy ship disappear into thin air?

According to a conspiracy theory, U.S. Navy members conducted a secret experiment. They wanted to make a ship called the USS *Eldridge* invisible to **radar**. The experiment went wrong, and the ship vanished from the naval shipyard in Philadelphia, Pennsylvania. It then appeared in Norfolk, Virginia, before reappearing back at the shipyard. Witnesses described a strange green-blue glow surrounding the ship just before it disappeared.

The USS *Eldridge* was a destroyer escort ship. It went on missions with other ships to help protect them.

NO PROOF

Although it's an interesting story, there is no proof the Philadelphia Experiment ever happened. A man named Carl M. Allen claimed to have been a witness from a nearby ship. But Allen was unable to provide any other evidence to support his claim. Another witness, Edward Dudgeon, served in the U.S. Navy aboard a ship in the Philadelphia naval yard. According to him, the *Eldridge* did have secret devices on board. But these devices were not able to make the ships invisible. Instead, they provided protection from magnetic **torpedoes**.

According to *The Philadelphia Inquirer* newspaper, several other sailors said the ship never docked in Philadelphia the day of the reported disappearance. The ship's log confirmed this.

Fact
Scientists think the reported blue-green glow near the *Eldridge* could have been St. Elmo's fire. In storms, electricity in the air can cause a bright blue glow around objects.

The U.S. Navy and the Office of Naval Research has officially stated that the Philadelphia Experiment never happened. They have researched their records and found no mention of the experiment. The Philadelphia Experiment is a conspiracy theory that some people believe, but it's not true.

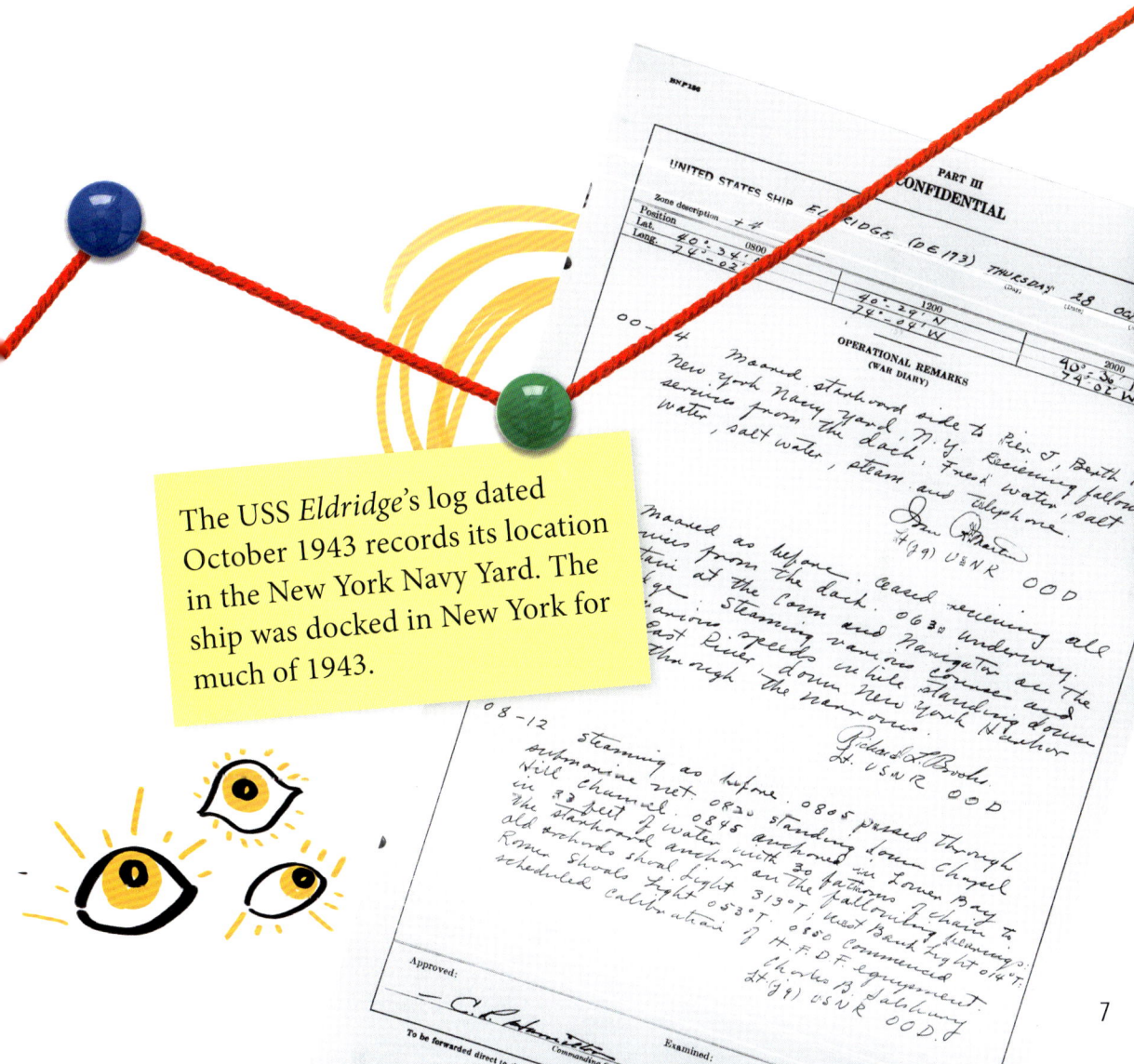

The USS *Eldridge*'s log dated October 1943 records its location in the New York Navy Yard. The ship was docked in New York for much of 1943.

SPOTLIGHT ON CONSPIRACY THEORIES

Conspiracy theories are stories or ideas that some people believe. They suggest that a **plot** is being carried out in secret. The government or powerful groups are often said to be involved. People think these groups are hiding something or secretly controlling events.

Sometimes conspiracy theories can be exciting because they offer different explanations to popular beliefs. However, it's important to remember that most conspiracy theories have been proven false by experts and scientists.

Many events in U.S. history have given rise to conspiracy theories. From secret plots to wartime attacks, let's investigate some of the most interesting and popular theories.

Questions to Ask About Conspiracy Theories

- When you find out about a conspiracy theory, do research. Learn as much as you can. It's important not to assume a conspiracy theory is true. Many conspiracy theories can be proven false. For others, parts of them may be true.
- What evidence supports this theory? Ask if there are reliable sources or scientific studies that provide evidence for the claims.
- Who is saying this? What are the sources of information? Consider whether the sources are trustworthy.
- Are there other explanations? Consider different viewpoints. Think critically and weigh different possibilities.
- Has this theory been widely accepted or rejected by experts? Understand the value of expert opinions and scientific evidence. Theories that are widely accepted by experts are generally more reliable than those supported by a few individuals or groups.

Chapter 2

THE ASSASSINATION OF JOHN F. KENNEDY

John F. Kennedy was the much-loved 35th president of the United States. At 43, he was the youngest person ever elected to the office. On November 22, 1963, he was riding in a car with his wife, Jacqueline, and others in Dallas, Texas. They were traveling in a planned route with other vehicles. People crowded along the streets to see the president. Suddenly, shots rang out. Two shots hit the president. He was rushed to the hospital. Soon after, he died. The horrific event shocked the nation.

President Kennedy (back seat, left) and his wife ride in the car November 22, 1963.

Lee Harvey Oswald's mug shot taken after his arrest

After the **assassination**, an investigation began. Lee Harvey Oswald was arrested for the crime. However, a man named Jack Ruby killed Oswald before he could be put on trial. Investigators did not find evidence that anyone else was involved.

A SECRET PLOT?

Some conspiracy theorists think that there was a plot to kill President Kennedy. They believe more people were involved. They don't think the government has provided the public with all the facts. Some point to the famous "grassy knoll" theory. According to this theory, there was a second shooter hiding on a grassy hill nearby. People say this second shooter fired the shot that killed the president. Conspiracy theorists say the movement of Kennedy's head back and to the left after being shot is consistent with the grassy knoll theory. Witnesses even reported hearing gunshots from the direction of the grassy knoll.

Fact

The bullet that hit Kennedy also hit and injured Texas Governor John Connally. Connally was riding in front of Kennedy.

The X on the street marks the spot where Kennedy was shot. Some people think there was an assassin near the grassy knoll's fenced area (left).

If more people were involved in the assassination, who were they? Conspiracy theorists have named many groups. The most common ones include the Central Intelligence Agency (CIA) and the **mob**. The Cuban and Soviet Union governments have also been suspected of being involved.

Members of the Warren Commission sit around a table in December 1963. The chairman was U.S. Chief Justice Earl Warren (middle).

SIFTING THROUGH EVIDENCE

An official group known as the Warren Commission conducted a thorough investigation of the assassination. The experts found no evidence to support any of the conspiracy theories. The Warren Commission concluded that Lee Harvey Oswald acted alone in shooting President Kennedy.

Later, another committee called the House Select Committee on Assassinations (HSCA) did another investigation. It also said Oswald shot the president, but it did not rule out the possibility of a plot. At the time, the committee was partly basing this conclusion on a sound recording from the day of the shooting. The shooting seemed to suggest there could have been multiple shooters. But afterward, this recording was largely discredited.

Oswald holds the same type of gun that was used to kill Kennedy. When shown this photo, Oswald said it was faked.

EXPERT STUDIES

Experts have also conducted several studies of the assassination. They have used models to show that Oswald shot the bullet that killed President Kennedy. Oswald was on the sixth floor of the Texas School Book Depository. The bullet's path lines up with this location. Experts also say Kennedy's head movements were consistent with a shot to the back of the head. Despite this evidence, many people still believe in conspiracy theories about President Kennedy's assassination.

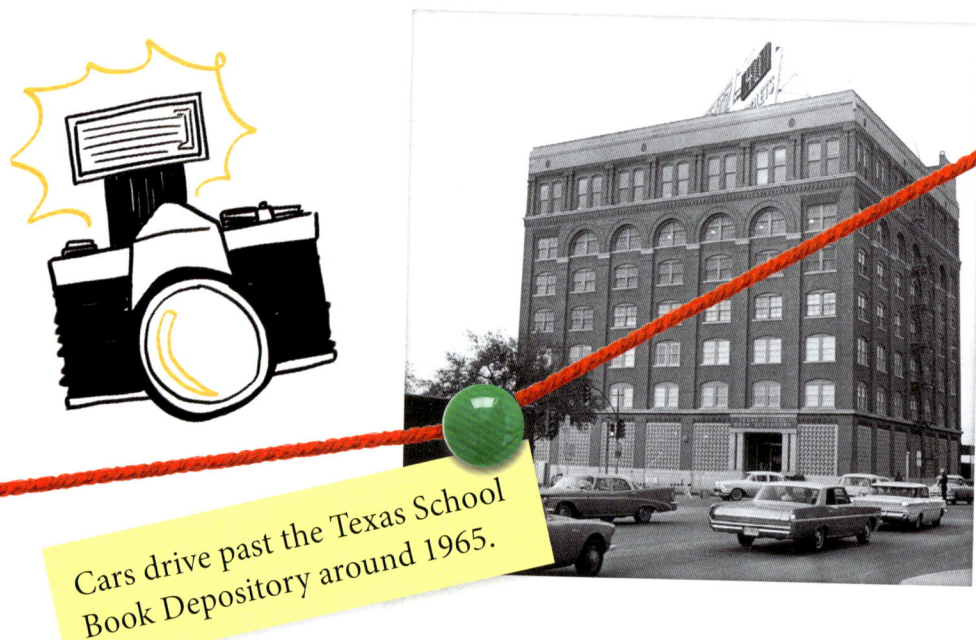

Cars drive past the Texas School Book Depository around 1965.

The Illuminati

Could a secret group called the Illuminati be controlling world events and governments behind the scenes? Some people think so. They say the goal of the group is to make a New World Order that would rule the whole planet. Some people have suggested that the Illuminati was responsible for the assassination of President Kennedy. Those who believe in the Illuminati say that their symbol is an eye set in a triangle. It is called the Eye of Providence. The symbol is also on the Great Seal of the United States and the U.S. one-dollar bill.

Chapter 3

THE ASSASSINATION OF DR. MARTIN LUTHER KING JR.

Dr. Martin Luther King Jr. was a famous civil rights leader in the United States. He fought for **equality** and justice for all people. He spoke out against **racism**. He believed peaceful **protests** would help achieve his goals.

On April 4, 1968, Dr. King was in Memphis, Tennessee. While on the balcony outside his motel room, he was shot and killed. This event shook the nation. The police began an investigation, and James Earl Ray was arrested for the crime. Police believed only he was involved in the shooting.

Dr. Martin Luther King Jr. waves to the crowd after giving his famous "I Have a Dream" speech in Washington, D.C., in 1963.

People gather outside the Lorraine Motel shortly after King was killed.

Fact

The motel that King was staying at when he was assassinated is now part of the National Civil Rights Museum. People can go there to learn about the civil rights movement and King's work.

However, conspiracy theorists believe that others were involved in his death. They say more individuals or groups were responsible for planning and carrying out the assassination. Many people did not support King's civil rights work. He had many enemies.

WHO COULD HAVE BEEN INVOLVED?

Some people even thought U.S. government groups could be involved. Because of his civil rights work, the Federal Bureau of Investigation (FBI) had been keeping track of King for many years. Officials thought he might have ties to **communism**. The U.S. government thought communism was a threat and wanted to limit its spread. King actually spoke out against communism. But the close watch the FBI kept on King led people to think the agency could have been involved in the assassination.

King (right) visited the FBI building to meet with FBI Director J. Edgar Hoover in 1964. They discussed issues related to his civil rights work.

James Earl Ray takes an oath before a committee after King's assassination.

Conspiracy theorists can give several reasons for their beliefs. After the assassination, Ray told many stories to try to prove his innocence. One of them was that he was set up by others. Ray said a man he knew only as Raoul was involved. In 1993, a Memphis bar owner named Loyd Jowers said he participated in a conspiracy to kill King. He said a mob member, the man named Raoul, and police officers were also involved.

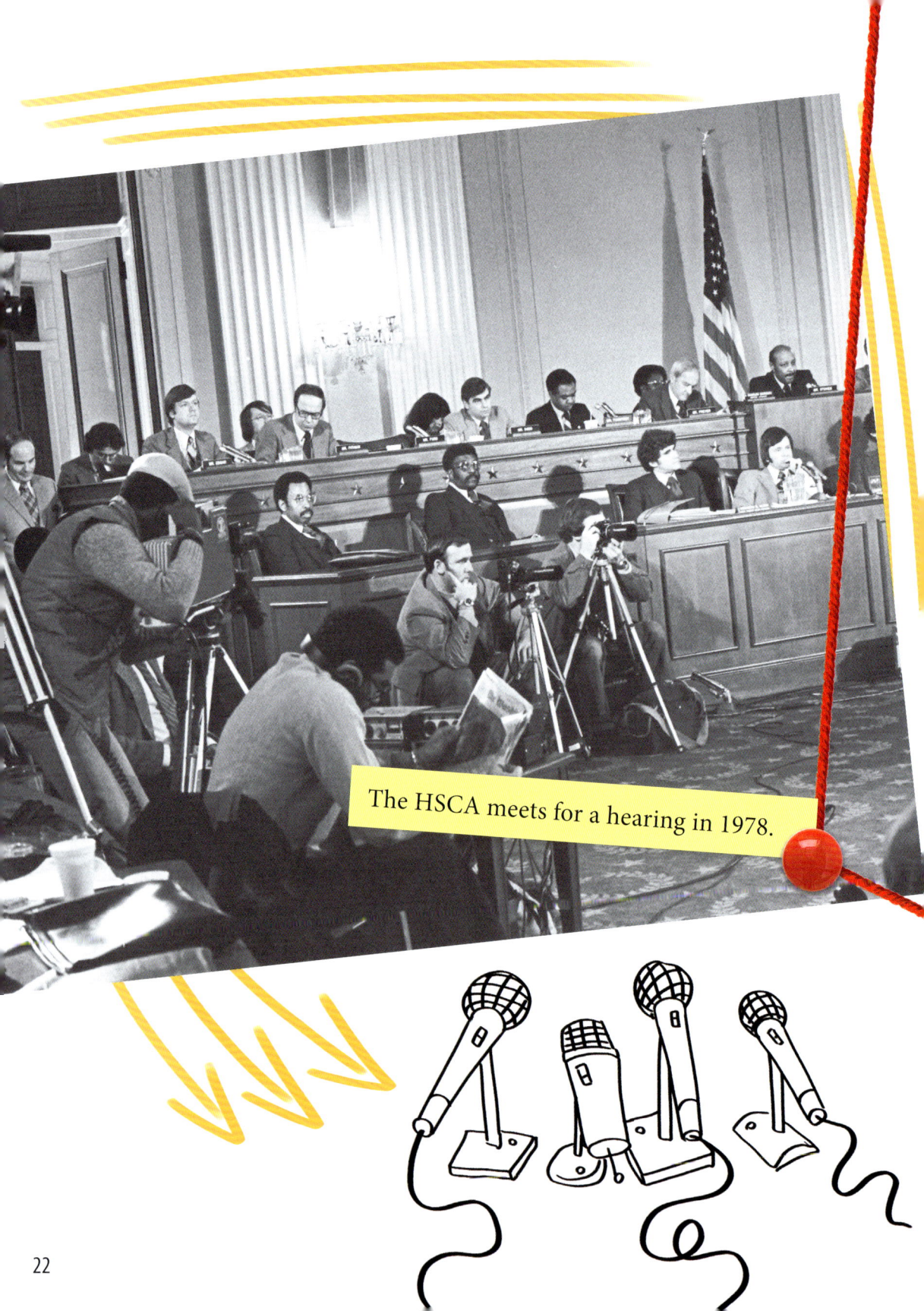
The HSCA meets for a hearing in 1978.

MANY INVESTIGATIONS

In 1978, the HSCA said that there could have been a conspiracy to kill King. It suggested Ray and his brothers may have committed the crime to collect money. They thought a **bounty** could have been put out for the killing of King. The HSCA did not find any evidence the FBI was involved.

The death of Martin Luther King Jr. has been officially investigated five times. All investigations have found that James Earl Ray shot Dr. King. Investigations did not find evidence that proved a larger conspiracy. They did not find Jowers to be credible because he had changed his story several times.

Chapter 4

THE PEARL HARBOR CONSPIRACY

In late 1941, World War II was raging around the world. The United States had remained neutral. U.S. leaders chose not to fight neither for the Allies nor the Axis powers. Pearl Harbor in Hawaii was the base for the U.S. Pacific Fleet. Most of the U.S. Navy's ships were docked there. On December 7, 1941, Japan launched a surprise air attack on the base. The attack left 2,403 Americans dead. It also crippled or destroyed eight battleships and more than 180 planes. This event caused America to join the war effort against the Axis powers, which included Japan, Germany, and Italy.

A conspiracy theory says that the U.S. government knew about the Pearl Harbor attack before it happened. However, officials allowed it to happen in order to give the U.S. a reason to join the war.

After the attack on Pearl Harbor, sailors attempted to rescue survivors.

Franklin D. Roosevelt

KEEPING SECRETS

Conspiracy theory believers claim that the U.S. president at the time, Franklin D. Roosevelt, knew the attack was coming. They say Pearl Harbor was an easy target because most of the U.S. Navy's ships were there. They also believe that there should have been no way to surprise American forces. According to them, Roosevelt must have made it possible for the Japanese to easily attack and destroy the U.S. Navy. They say Roosevelt wanted to go to war. Believers in the conspiracy theory say commanders weren't properly warned about a possible attack.

INVESTIGATION FINDINGS

The U.S. Congress launched an investigation into the attack. It found U.S. intelligence agencies knew that the Japanese were planning on moving into the South Pacific. The government sent a war warning to Pacific commanders Husband Kimmel and Walter Short on November 27. This was 10 days before the attack. It said war could happen at any time.

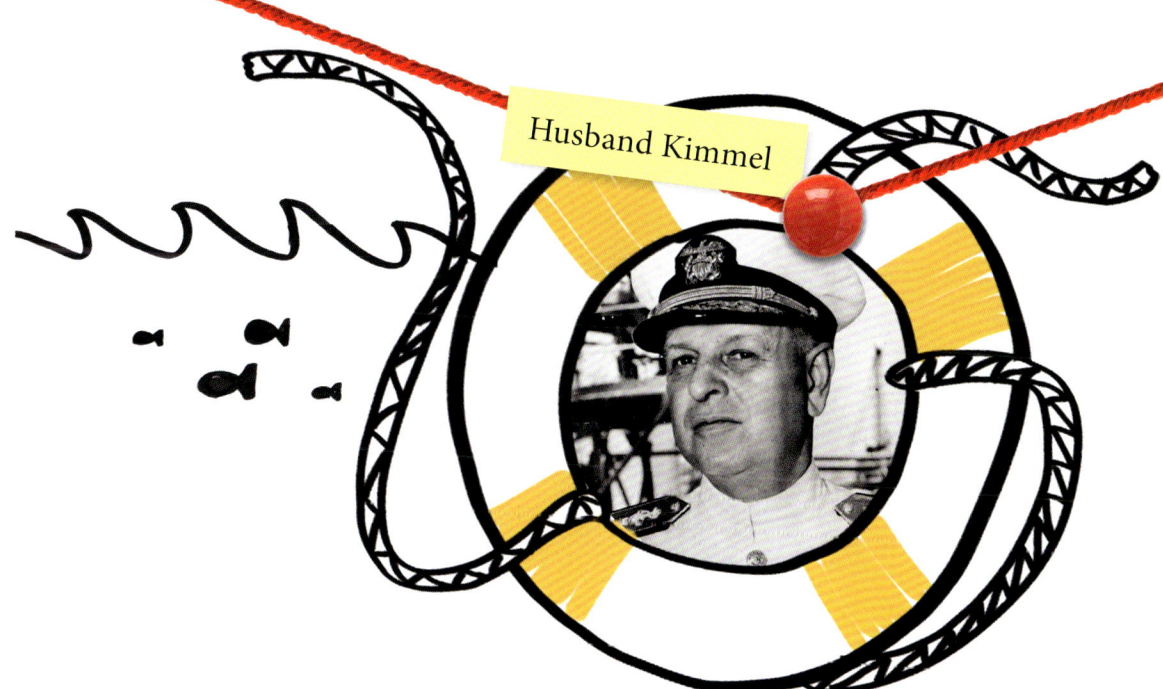

Husband Kimmel

The destructive attack on Pearl Harbor is remembered as an important event of World War II.

No evidence has been discovered that proves U.S. military leaders or Roosevelt knew for certain the attack was coming. Information was passed on to naval commanders. They didn't take the warning seriously. They may have believed an attack would happen elsewhere. Roosevelt did not want Japan to keep taking over territory. But there isn't proof he wanted to go to war.

Enemy Planes on Radar

Evidence revealed there was a chance for the U.S. to be more prepared for the attack. A radar operator reported seeing planes on his screen early the morning of December 7, 1941. An officer told him not to worry about it. As a result, the warning was not passed on.

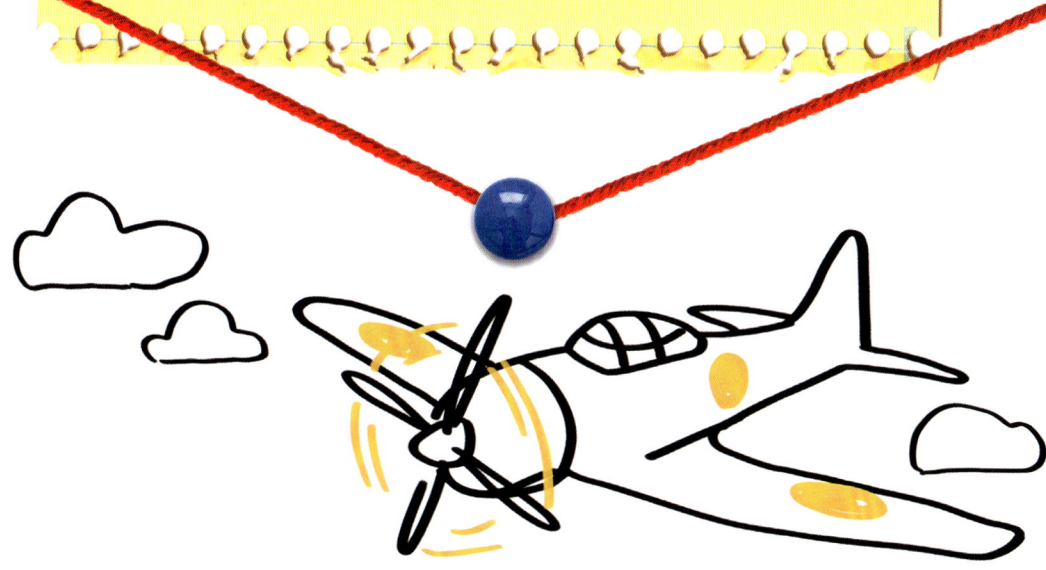

Conspiracy theories related to the history of the United States are fascinating to think about. However, it is important to research information thoroughly. Conspiracy theories often lack strong evidence. Most have been proven wrong by experts.

Glossary

assassination (uh-sah-suh-NAY-shuhn)—the murder of someone who is well known or important

bounty (BAUN-tee)—money paid for the killing or capture of a person or animal

communism (KAHM-yuh-ni-zuhm)—system in which goods and property are owned by the government and shared in common

equality (i-KWAH-luh-tee)—the same rights for everyone

mob (MOB)—a criminal organization

plot (PLOT)—a secret plan

protest (PROH-test)—an organized public event to show strong disapproval of something

racism (RAY-sih-zuhm)—the belief that one race is better than another race

radar (RAY-dar)—a device that uses radio waves to track the location of objects

torpedo (tor-PEE-doh)—an underwater missile

Read More

Berglund, Bruce. *The Assassination of President John F. Kennedy: A Day That Changed America.* North Mankato, MN: Capstone, 2023.

Fowler, Natalie. *A Pearl Harbor Time Capsule: Artifacts of the Surprise Attack on the U.S.* North Mankato, MN: Capstone, 2021.

Jackson, Tom. *Fake News.* Mission Viejo, CA: QED Publishing, 2020.

Internet Sites

Kiddle: Assassination of John F. Kennedy Facts for Kids
kids.kiddle.co/Assassination_of_John_F._Kennedy

National Geographic Kids: Attack on Pearl Harbor
kids.nationalgeographic.com/history/article/pearl-harbor

What Is the True Story of the Philadelphia Experiment?
discoveryuk.com/mysteries/what-is-the-true-story-of-the-philadelphia-experiment

Index

Allen, Carl M., 6
Allies, 4, 24

Central Intelligence Agency (CIA), 13
civil rights, 18, 19, 20
communism, 20

Dudgeon, Edward, 6

Eldridge, 4, 5, 6, 7

Federal Bureau of Investigation (FBI), 20, 23

"grassy knoll" theory, 12

House Select Committee on Assassinations (HSCA), 15, 22, 23

Illuminati, 17

Japan, 24, 28

Kennedy, John F., 10, 12, 13, 14, 15, 16, 17
King, Martin Luther, Jr., 18, 19, 20, 21, 23

Oswald, Lee Harvey, 11, 14, 15, 16

Pearl Harbor, 24, 25, 26, 28
protests, 18

Ray, James Earl, 18, 21, 23
Roosevelt, Franklin D., 26, 28

Texas School Book Depository, 16

U.S. Navy, 4, 6, 7, 24, 26

Warren Commission, 14

About the Author

Dr. Phill Simpson is an award-winning author of many novels, chapter books, and other books for children. He has also written more than 100 books for the global education market. Phill holds a Masters in Creative Writing and a Doctorate in Education.

When he's not writing, he works as an elementary school teacher and educational consultant. Phill lives and writes in Auckland, New Zealand, with his wife Rose, their son, Jack, and their two border terriers, Whiskey and Raffles.